Clicker Training for
Clever Cats

Clicker Training for
Clever Cats

Learning can be fun!

By Martina Braun

CADMOS

Contents

Contents

Introduction

The fact of having picked up this book suggests that you are an open-minded person who is willing to experiment. Regardless of all the scepticism regarding the training of cats, you have let yourself in for the adventure of getting to know what working with a clicker is like, and entering a closer relationship with your cat at the same time. I can assure you of this: you will not regret it. The clicker is more than a learning aid; it is a tool which enables us humans to enter into a multi-layered, completely new kind of communication with our cats. Maybe you will employ the clicker in order to teach your cat things that you find desirable for your life together, or perhaps you want your cat to 'unlearn' some unpleasant habits, or just want to use the clicker for fun and entertainment: the possibilities are endless!

I'm very pleased to be able to guide you across the tip of an iceberg, to be able to show you its hills and hollows, nooks and crannies. It is up to you how deep you want to delve to discover what else is slumbering under

Pretending to be a dangerous tiger – Mowgli does this to perfection by following the target stick with his paws.

Getting there is not that difficult at all! With the aid of the target stick, even the slightest indication of spontaneous behaviour is affirmed.

the surface. There need be no limits to your imagination.

I promise not to bore you with theory for too long, but please allow me just one remark regarding the term 'upbringing'. To me, 'upbringing' implies hard work: it requires effort to 'bring someone up'. Sometimes more, sometimes less. It is exactly for this reason that, in my view, the word is not appropriate. You will find that with a clicker, no effort is required to teach your cat 'sit' or 'go into the cat basket'. The animal acts on his own accord. All you need is patience in order to allow the cat to try out for himself what is desired and what isn't, a keen eye for the cat's reactions and the behaviour he is offering to you, and the understanding that there are a few differences between the training of cats and the training of dogs.

Dealing with a dog you can say: 'Right Bonzo, I have a bit of time to spare, let's do some clicker exercises.' With a cat, the cat will say: 'Well, my dear tin-opener, I think I can spare you a little time now. You may get the clicker out for me.'

How does the cat get to know the clicker?

There is a learning method that no mammal – not even humans! – can ignore: classical conditioning. It is the basis for clicker training, and the way it works is in fact incredibly simple. Take the following example: imagine you have been out on a very hot day. You are sweating, completely over-heated and

you have an incredible thirst. Just as you walk through the front door you hear someone in the kitchen opening a bottle of pop with a refreshing fizz! I can vividly picture your eager anticipation of a large, thirst-quenching gulp as you rush into the kitchen. Why? Because you know the noise that a bottle of pop makes when it's being opened, and in your mind this is 'conditioned' with the terms: 'drink – cool – refreshing – thirst-quenching'. Had you never heard this fizzing sound before, it would have no meaning for you. Or in other words, the fizzing noise of the bottle of pop would be a neutral stimulus for you.

With this process in mind, we are ready to begin classically conditioning our cat – to use the expert expression. If you make a click in front of your cat at home, using a clicker from the pet shop, this will be a neutral sound for the cat without any relevance or meaning. In order for the click (the neutral stimulus) to assume a meaning for the cat, and to become the subject of positive associations for him, we have only to observe one small basic rule: timing!

Timing

The cat gets a treat immediately after the click. The 'immediately after' is the most important part of the whole affair. The treat must not be given at exactly the same time as the clicking sound, because then no association would take place. The cat will only concentrate on the treat, and the clicking sound will make no impact. If, on the other hand, the period of time elapsing between the clicking sound and the giving of the treat is too long, you will also fail to achieve a conditioning effect, because the animal cannot make a connection between the click and the treat.

Ideally, there should be a time span of between one fifth of a second and half a second maximum between the click and the treat.

So you take the new clicker in your hand, put a few treats easy to reach nearby, and call your cat towards you. Only click once each time, and give him the treat within half a second. Repeat this a few times. And whether you believe it, or not, you are well on your way to classically conditioning your cat! It is possible that the cat will just run away after a

The reward for good work can consist of a cuddle or a loving nose-butt as well.

few treats. That doesn't matter at all! Remember, for each training session:

➤ To click once at the correct time is better and more valuable than 20 clicks at the wrong time!

This is the correct sequence:

➤ A click followed by a reward within half a second at the most.

Repeat this initial exercise two to three times a day for a maximum of two to five minutes on each occasion. Within a short period of time you will notice that your cat has made a connection between the click and the treat. The more frequently you click at the start, the stronger the cat will be conditioned to believe that the click will be followed by something positive. We will talk later about the reasons why you should not use the clicker to coax or call your cat to come towards you. But in order to make this first success more apparent to you, you can carry out the following test, but please only do it this once! After two days' initial work with the clicker, and while your cat is nearby and awake, just click on the clicker once. You will find that your cute little kitty will come eagerly running towards you in anticipation of a treat. Congratulations! You have already taken the most important step!

Classical conditioning

You have just grasped the principle behind one of the most important commonly effective learning methods, whose discovery we owe to the Russian scientist Ivan Petrovitsch Pavlov

(1849–1936); this is classical conditioning, the basic characteristics of which can be summed up as follows:

With the use of correct timing, the animal cannot evade the effects of conditioning, because the reaction that follows is not guided or affected by the individual's own free will, but rather it is subject to physiological processes. This means that the animal cannot influence this process by its behaviour.

This way an originally neutral stimulus (the click) becomes associated with a positive stimulus (food/play/cuddle), and takes on the same meaning.

An example of this process is that every cat who loves his moist food will react to the noise that's made by opening the aluminium tray or tin. Unintentionally, a classical conditioning has already taken place here. The 'natural reward' – in this case the food – is called the 'primary reinforcer'. The sound of the tin being opened is called the 'secondary reinforcer'. That's why in the context of working with a clicker we talk about the deployment of a 'secondary reinforcer'. The anticipation of food or treats is reinforced or, in other words, announced by the clicker.

Next to the treat this is one of the nicest affirmations.   *Playing as a reward! With the speedy 'Cat-dancer'.*

The clicker works for all cats

Deaf, blind, fat, thin, fussy eaters, young or old, indoor or outdoor cats – clicker training works for every cat. I can well imagine that some readers will be tempted to put the book to one side now, saying: 'My cat wouldn't lift a finger for a treat.' Please continue reading all the same! Because the primary reinforcer which we need in order to subsequently reinforce it with the clicker doesn't necessarily have to be food-related. It could be anything which represents a genuine, direct reward for the cat. It could just as easily consist of a playing session with the cat's favourite toy, but also a cuddle and tender words for the little moggy, ever in need of love and attention. What's important here is

Isn't this a lot of fun!

Of course, at the end of the game the cat has to win!

this: make the beloved toy disappear afterwards, so it doesn't lose its charm. And precede every cuddling session with a small clicker exercise to make it clear to the cat that the cuddle is a reward.

To keep things simple in this context I will just talk about treats or rewards. But even if you have a cat who prefers to be rewarded with food, there may sometimes be situations where a rumbustious playing session would represent the bigger reward. Whatever emphasises the effect of the clicker, whatever the cat likes best at this point in time, is suitable as a primary reinforcer.

Now there will be those amongst you who will voice concerns regarding kitty's potential weight gain from all those tasty treats, as a result of working with the clicker.

'Lift the right paw'

'Lift the left paw'

'Gimme five' Anima is the 'paw specialist', and is losing 40 grams per week due to the various exercises. By doing this she has lost a half a kilogram already.

I would like to share a few thoughts with you in this regard. I often wonder where the idea has originated that cats should always have unlimited access to their food? Many fussy eaters would have far better appetite levels if they weren't constantly overwhelmed on a daily basis by overly abundant offers of food. By keeping to fixed feeding times, free-roaming cats can be trained to develop a marvellous home-coming rhythm. (Of course a cat won't return home punctually always and every day, just more often!) And many cats who have constant access to food day and night on a self-serve basis pay dearly for this luxury with diseases of the urinary tract. The cat's bloodstream needs the occasional break between meals to return to its resting metabolism. During the intake of food, cats' urine is more alkaline. Now it is very important to have acid urine, because the acidity helps dissolve bladder and kidney stones. In a cat who has free access to something to nibble at all times, the urine never turns acidic, but remains alkaline, potentially promoting urinary tract diseases.

We tend to forget that our cats still carry the inheritance of the African wild cat in their genes. As ambush hunters, they are used to sitting in front of a mousehole for hours on end, until the time has come to pounce. So why should it not be possible for a cat in a domestic situation to wait until meal time? Feral cats only know one logic: a full stomach has to be earned beforehand.

So why do we condemn our cats to idleness? Have your cat 'sing for his dinner', and you will enhance your relationship with him. One prerequisite for the clicker training is of course to ensure that you will no longer give in to conventional begging at the table. From now on, for every click (and the subsequent reward), the cat has to keep his part of the bargain. A little consistency on our part is needed to make clicker training work. I realise that after achieving one 'sit' you won't have the feeling that your cat has actually learned something. But I promise, he has indeed! It is very exciting for cats when they realise that they can influence our actions by their own. You will find that your moggy will be more balanced, more awake and less bored as a result. I can assure you from the experiences I have had in my clinic, that boredom is often at the root of behavioural problems among cats. You will be able to read elsewhere in this book how boredom can be averted with the aid of a clicker – or to put it differently: by assigning cats tasks!

Or are you the owner of a 'purr generator' who is more or less overweight already? In this case you have probably already tried various diets without success? Mmmh, that's something I can relate to! In this case we will begin today, here and now, to click your cat into shape! By making the cat 'earn' each lump of food individually, the feeding process takes up more time, making each morsel more precious, and it is possible to surreptitiously reduce the total amount of food. (Please don't pursue this with too much fervour! For a healthy slimming regime with a chance of enduring success, the cat must not be allowed to lose more than 100 grams per week!)

You can even use clicker training on cats who are deaf. The primary reinforcer stays the same, that's the food, the cuddle or play. As a secondary reinforcer you simply have to substitute the clicker (audible reinforcer) with a small torch (visual reinforcer). Instead of a verbal prompt, you give a visual sign to your cat, for example by lifting the index finger of the left hand, in order to signal 'sit' to the cat. Deaf cats are particularly accomplished at interpreting body signals.

Blind cats can be taught various things with a clicker by utilising spontaneous behaviour displayed by the cat. In the chapter on 'Targeting' you can read how to teach a blind cat to touch a pointing stick and to follow it, so you can guide and lead him by employing very simple means.

Young cats are naturally curious and keen to learn. They can undergo clicker training from an early age. However, you need to make some allowances for the fact that young cats are easily distracted, and that it is possible a kitten may break off a session because of a leaf sailing by, or a fly buzzing on the window.

For old cats who frequently suffer from a decline of their powers, working with the clicker is a marvellous method that allows them to experience success and fulfilment. Even if the cat only comes into contact with the clicker for the first time in his dotage – it's never too late!

A conventional clicker, available from any pet shop.

The slightly newer generation of clickers has an action button permitting exact timing.

Does it have to be a clicker?

No, it doesn't, actually. But as we have already learnt, the aspect of timing is very important, and we have to be able to react very quickly. The clicker makes a brief, succinct sound and is therefore well suited for this purpose. What is also important is the fact that the sound we want to use as a secondary reinforcer is not one which constantly occurs in the context of everyday life. After all the click is supposed to be a signal! If instead of the click we were to employ words such as 'good!', 'great!' or 'yes!', we would not be able to preclude the possibility of these words being used in a different context which doesn't concern the training of your cat at all.

There are numerous versions of the clicker: a little plastic box with a metal plate inside which makes the typical clicking sound when pushed, or the old metal clicker frog you may remember from your childhood. There are decorative wooden versions and adjustable three-tone-clickers which give off a slightly different sound on each setting. It doesn't really matter which model you go for. The important thing is that the sound thus produced will not scare the animal. If your cat is extremely sensitive to sounds, I'd recommend that you substitute the clicking of a ballpoint pen at the beginning. For some of my cat patients, the 'clicker' consists of a rapid rap with a finger on the table. Whichever type of clicker you finally plump for, the sound has to be brief, quick and unusual.

The first steps:
Affirming and naming spontaneous behaviour

'Sit!'

Having successfully conditioned the cat to react to the clicker, we will begin to affirm spontaneously displayed behaviour. Take the following situation: it is meal time and your cat shows signs of being hungry. A fabulous opportunity to teach your moggy how to do 'sit'! Prepare the meal, take the clicker in your hand and wait to see what your cat will do next. He may go around your legs, looking up to you as if to ask: 'What's up?

Is dinner finally ready?' Maybe he'll miaow or get on his hind legs up against you. Please don't say a word, and don't stare at your cat. Just wait patiently and bide your time. It is very important that you don't talk, thereby avoiding superfluous signals. There would be no point saying 'Sit!' at this point. The cat doesn't yet understand this request and has to learn what it means first. At some point – probably with an air of indignation – your little darling will sit down in front of you.

This is exactly the moment when you have to make the click! It is the very moment when the cat is carrying out the act of sitting down. Immediately follow this click with a reward. For this first step the procedure is as follows:

➤ Sitting down action +
   simultaneous click > reward

Now your cat is sitting in front of you in eager anticipation. Take one or two steps to one side, in order to make the cat give up his seated position and get up again. Wait. As soon as the cat makes the first move in order to sit down again, you make another click and give him a reward. With a bit of luck you can repeat this sequence of events a few times. Finish the exercise with a 'jackpot', putting the rest of the meal on the floor in front of him, just as you would usually. Even with this small exercise you will find after repeating it just a few times that the cat will have understood and will sit down in front of you in anticipation of his meal. Once the cat knows what to expect, only then has the time come to give the whole thing a name.

In practice this will look like this: Tiddles comes sauntering into the kitchen in order to collect his dinner. You are wellprepared, with food and clicker, and as your cat is about to sit down, you ask him to do so in a friendly tone of voice: 'Tiddles, sit!' The moment the cat sits down you work the clicker (the click ends the action!) and quickly follow this with the reward. Bravo! You have taught your cat to do 'sit'! Now the sequence is as follows:

➤ Sitting down action + simultaneous
   command > end action + click > reward

If you have carried out this exercise in the living room, for example, it is possible that your cat will run off after the click and speedily head towards the kitchen. That's all right. He has understood that the click is followed by a treat. It's just force of habit that's making him run towards the kitchen, because that's where every meal had been served in the past. Follow him and give him his well-deserved reward.

Later, after you have achieved a certain amount of routine, only give the command 'Sit!' before the cat sits down. From this moment onwards, at which this command has definitely been added, understood and carried out, it is important to only give the cat a click for the sitting-down action you have requested, and no longer when the cat has sat down by coincidence, without being prompted. By doing this the 'command', the word 'sit', becomes as important to the reward as the click or the treat. Finally the sequence is:

➤Command 'Sit!' > action by the cat
> click > reward

If your goal is to have your cat do 'sit' anywhere, and not just in one particular place, you just have to repeat this exercise in various locations (in the kitchen, in the living room, on the balcony …). And I bet it has taken you only two or three days to get to this stage!

If you have trained your cat with a word that turns out not to be practical in the end, because there is the danger of a mix-up, or because it is used in everyday speech too frequently (such as, for example the word 'Come!'), and you want to change it to a different word later, you need to always say the new command before the previous command, and do this until the new command (for example 'Here!') has become part of the routine. Finally you can leave out the old command ('Come!') completely.

➤Command 'Here!' > command 'Come!'
> cat's action > click > reward

You can deliberately train every action that your cat performs of his own free will by affirming this action when it is displayed by coincidence. Then, after the cat has understood what he is expected to do, you can assign a name to the action. Examples for this could be: 'Lie down!', 'Jump up!' (perhaps onto a chair?), 'Jump off!' (off the dinner table?), 'Roll!', 'Catch!' (the furry toy mouse or the tennis ball) or 'Call!', affirming the cat's miaow. Particularly with regard to free-roaming cats, I find it very handy if the cat has learned how to respond vocally. Imagine your little gypsy doesn't come home on time and you are going out to search for him. Many cats find themselves locked in cellars and garages but merely listen silently to their humans calling them. Wouldn't it be helpful, in this situation, if you were able to hear a miaow and find your little dare-devil a little more quickly?

It is important, however, that you don't become too ambitious as a result of enjoying your successes. Don't take the next step until the cat has understood the previous step one hundred per cent, otherwise these exercises end in frustration for both parties – human and cat – and the sense of fun is lost.

'Roll!'

Some actions, such as, for example, 'rolling', which involves the cat rolling around on his back, although performed spontaneously, will only be displayed in very particular situations, for instance when the cat is very relaxed. In order to support this action with a clicker, it would be essential to have it close to hand at all times (perhaps in your trouser pocket) so that you can react quickly enough. Once your cat has been conditioned to react to the clicker, it won't matter very much if, after the 'click', you have to walk to the kitchen first in order to fetch the reward. Keeping to the half-second interval between the click and the reward is only absolutely crucial at the beginning – during the conditioning. Afterwards the clicker sound assumes equal importance with the subsequent reward.

'Lie down!'

If you want to teach your cat to 'lie down', sound the clicker even at the smallest indication of this behaviour. Let's suppose your cat has learnt 'Sit!' and is now waiting for the click and his treat. Because cats are incredibly persistent, he will sooner or later crouch down with an air of defiance, if the expected affirmation does not follow – and

'click'! This movement of crouching down is going in the direction of lying down, that's why you make the click. Clearly define for yourself what 'lying down' involves. The cat is on the floor (or on a chair), with his tummy touching the ground, the hind legs are under the body and the front paws usually more or less extended in front of him. Crouching down is part of the process of lying down, hence the affirmation. The cat has only

With a treat that is moved slowly on the floor away from the cat, the first moves towards a lying-down position are affirmed.

During the second step, a crouching-down position has already been assumed …

… and in the end the 'lying down' is working perfectly well.

crouched down because he is waiting and perhaps a little frustrated, because sitting down has not earned him a click. Once he realises that it's the crouching down that gets an affirmation now, he will lie down voluntarily, and we are already where we wanted to be: 'lying down'.

You also can train two behaviours at the same time. For many cats this will actually be necessary, because they learn very quickly and start getting bored just as easily. Be careful, however, to make sure that the actions are very distinct in order to avoid manoeuvring the cat in an undesired direction. Therefore I would recommend never to train 'sit' and 'lie down' at the same time. Your cat may end up thinking that he is supposed to do nothing but sit and lie down all the time, and he might end up becoming practically stationary. Or in the opposite case, if you only use the clicker for an exercise which aims at an action and never a resting position, the cat may become hyperactive as a result. The best would be to combine a calm exercise – such as the 'Sit' – with an action – such as 'Jump up!', working on both exercises simultaneously.

Changing locations

The cat learns by making an association between coincidences. For the proper reinforcement of learned actions it is therefore important to repeat them again and again in different locations, because the location of the action also has to be included in this process of association. Your cat may end up being able to carry out the command 'Sit!' in the living room only, because this is where it has always been practised. Therefore it is important to carry out these exercises in different parts of the house. As the cat becomes better at mastering an action, he will be less susceptible to any distractions, such as practising on the balcony, in the garden, or in the evening with visitors present. Your super-cat will condescendingly allow you to show off your newly acquired skills of using the clicker at the right moment.

Operant conditioning

We have now advanced to the second basic learning method for clicker training: operant (or instrumental) conditioning.

This learning principle applies to all mammals and was researched by the American psychologist Burrhus Frederik Skinner (1904–1990). It sounds complicated, but in practice it is really simple:

The cat learns that his behaviour influences whatever is going to happen next. Accordingly he can effect positive consequences (food, cuddles or play) by his own behaviour, but also avoid negative ones (for example not being given any attention, or being ignored). When we talk about a behaviour being 'reinforced', we mean that it is displayed more frequently.

For example by sitting down a cat can effect having a click and a treat given to him. If he doesn't sit, he doesn't get anything. As soon as a cat has understood that he himself can influence whether he will get a treat or not, he will increasingly carry out the action (in our case, 'sit') required to get a treat.

In order to further clarify this learning principle to you, here is an example which many cat owners will already be acquainted with. Your cat wakes you up with loud miaows every morning at six o'clock because he is hungry. You have experienced that the cat will not stop until you have got up and given him some food. So you drag yourself out of bed, stagger into the kitchen in a daze, and fill the empty food bowl with alacrity. You have been subject to perfect operant conditioning by your cat! (If this describes you, below under the heading 'Stay!' you'll find a suggestion as to how to resolve this situation.)

The shaping of behaviour

Your cat now does 'Sit!' and 'Lie down!', which will be a source of considerable bafflement for some of your friends, and which will make even some dog owners go green with envy. You are rightfully proud. But now you would like your cat to learn 'Lie down – stay!'. He is not just supposed to lie down, but must remain lying down and not get up again straight away. We achieve this by shaping. Shaping means that a behaviour is

shaped, or in other words only the best execution of a behaviour is rewarded. The criteria for this are established beforehand by yourself. You'll need just a bit more information for this.

The click is the signal which ends an action. This is very important! Up to now we have ended the action which was in the process of being carried out with a click, and afterwards there was an immediate reward. Now we want to shape the desired behaviour according to the criteria that the cat should lie down and stay lying down for a certain period of time, so the click to end the action should occur later.

'Stay!'

Start with the normal 'lying down' exercise. Observe how long the cat will stay lying down on his own accord by counting quietly. Let's assume that he remains in the lying down position for four seconds before getting up again. Now we have a starting point. Four seconds is the status quo. Next time when you do the lying down exercise, you already know that your cat will in all probability get up after four seconds. Ask the cat to lie down, but this time quietly count from the moment your cat is about to lie down, and click only after three seconds. Follow this with the treat immediately. We have lowered the initial measurement on purpose, because we are dealing with an estimate here, and we also have to factor in our own reaction time. The important thing is that the cat gets his click while still in a lying-down position. It would be wrong to make the click at the moment when the cat is about to get up again. If you have missed that moment, don't click after the event, 'just to make sure'.

Don't hold your cat down, and don't scream 'Stop! No! Stay down!' Just start from the beginning – straight away or maybe in a few hours; you have a whole (feline) lifetime to get it right!

Once you have succeeded in clicking after three seconds have passed, and while the cat was still lying down every time, in the next round of this exercise try to extend the time before the click to four seconds. Five seconds the next day, then seven, ten, and so on. But please don't become too obsessed with these figures! As soon as your cat has understood that all he needs to do is to lie there and wait for the click and the treat to arrive, you will be able to increase the time spent in the 'stay' position in large increments. If you notice that your cat can never wait, and always gets up too soon, this is a sure sign that you have expected too much too quickly of your cat. In this case, you start the exercise from the stage when things were still going swimmingly, and this time increase the time spent in 'stay' in smaller steps.

You can do this exercise anywhere in the home, or in a particular place. If you want to stop your cat begging at the table, for instance, and in order to get his click and a treat, have him lying in a particular place until the humans have finished their meal. Or you may want to teach your rumbustuous, fidgety tom-cat to lie down and calmly wait until you have put his collar on him, so he may go on his daily excursion. In this case the sequence of events would be: Command 'Lie down – stay!' > put cat collar on > click and reward. The reward in this case may be unlocking the cat flap instead of the treat. For a tom-cat who is impatiently looking forward to his daily walk, this is at least as valuable.

Are you one of those involuntary early risers who are forced out of their warm beds each morning by their determined cat? From now on, the little darling will only get his food if he is sitting in a specific place, for example on a stool or a chair in the kitchen. Now you can shape this behaviour regarding the duration, i.e. how long the cat will stay sitting down. You proceed as described above in tiny little increments. Thus the cat will learn: 'I'll only get fed if I sit on this stool.' I'd even recommend you to make the criteria more specific. The cat will only get his food if he sits on the stool quietly, without uttering a miaow. Now you just have to be very consistent and never, I repeat, never(!) give in to your cat again, when he approaches your bed whining and miaowing. This requires some patience on your part; your persistence has to exceed that of your cat, if only by a tiny margin. But it will be worth it.

Whichever behaviour you would like to shape, it should never involve more than one criterion at once! Clearly define to yourself what you want from your cat. Your cat will only learn to understand what it is you want to train, if you're quite clear about it yourself.

Speedy execution

If you have got the idea that your cat should sit down, and stay sitting down, but you want him to sit down quickly as well, you have three criteria to deal with.

Begin with the criterion which involves the cat sitting down quickly, and proceed as described above. You first observe how long the cat usually takes until he has sat down. Give the command and start counting quietly, until the cat has definitely assumed a sitting-down position. You measure the status quo, and from this point onwards you only give a click to executions which are quicker than your first counted measurement.

One piece of advice: whenever you are trying to achieve an action to be executed speedily, you should integrate this criterion at an early stage. To train for speed afterwards is very difficult, because the cat has already learnt that he will get a click, no matter whether he takes his time lying down, or does it quickly.

Once you have taught your cat how to sit down and how to sit down quickly, then you concentrate on the criterion 'stay sitting down'. While doing this you can neglect the 'sitting down quickly' a little. What kitty has learnt once he doesn't forget that quickly. Again, you always reward the best 'staying in a sitting position'. After the cat has learnt this, you combine the separate criteria. Only then the complete sequence of events is given a click: sitting down quickly and staying in a sitting down position. You proceed in the same manner if you want to shape the cri-terion of the 'location'. First give a click to the voluntary sitting down, or the early stages of the sitting-down movement, later specifically the sitting down following a command, and then only the sitting in a place of your choice.

Grooming and other inconveniences

You can also use the shaping method when you want to teach your cat to allow you to comb and brush him. Begin by giving your cat a click for slightly touching his back with your hand. For this the cat should be sitting or lying down, and not be displaying any signs of distrust. Go to the next level by taking a brush or a comb, show this to the cat, and then briefly touch the cat's back with the back of the brush (bristles or teeth pointing upwards). Each touch is then followed by a click or a treat. Gently run the back of the brush or comb, little by little, further and further over the cat's back. As soon as the cat stays calmly sitting down, allowing you to slide the back of the brush or comb over his coat, you begin to do the same exercise using the bristles or teeth side. First just one touch, then you increase this gradually from a simple touch to finally brushing and combing. Finally the cat only gets a click when the grooming has been completed. Sensitive parts of the body have to be treated separately, step by step affirm-ing the acceptance of the tiniest touch, as described above.

For clipping the claws, you follow the same procedure. Lightly touch the paw with your finger. Every passive response by your cat receives a click. Be careful not to click if your cat withdraws his paw or starts rumbling.

Increase the duration by leaving your fingers on the cat's paw for several seconds. Then you gradually begin to take the paw into your hand and gently extend the claws. Make a click every time your cat allows you to do

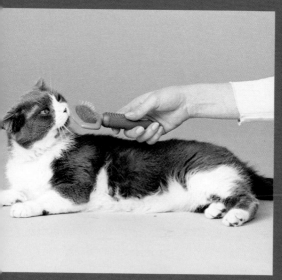

Slowly getting used to grooming with the back of the brush.

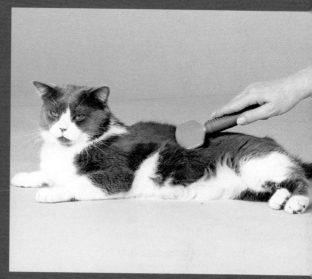

Through step-by-step training, the brushing can be enjoyed unreservedly.

If the reward consists of a great excursion, the harness isn't such a bother after all!

Mowgli has learned to love his collar in much the same way.

something – including clipping the claws. Thus every clipped claw is followed by a click; by the end of the training, you only give a click when the complete paw has been manicured.

You can use the same sensitive method to get your cat used to wearing a collar or harness, or to tolerate being picked up and carried.

Avoiding mistakes creeping in

To avoid right from the start mistakes creeping in, and you and your cat losing your motivation as a result, please always bear in mind:

1. Don't expect too much too soon! Your cat will not be able to attain the optimum accomplished behaviour overnight. At the beginning, every approximation to the desired behaviour should be rewarded. Then gradually, step by step, the optimum version of the behaviour is shaped from this. So at the beginning, your cat will not sit on command. We quickly take advantage of a situation when the cat is sitting down of his own accord and affirm this by a click. Or the cat indicates that he intends to sit down. Then even the first sign of the intention gets a click.

No other learning method leaves the cat as much freedom to do what he likes; but he will only get an affirmation for displaying a behaviour that is desired by us. If the cat displays a behaviour that is not desired by us, this will simply be ignored. The cat learns quickly that a reward will only be forthcoming when it has been preceded by a click. And he learns that, by his behaviour, he can influence whether he'll get a click or not! Once he has grasped this concept, he will increasingly display those behaviours voluntarily, because experience has taught him that they will be rewarded with a click. The cat will start to become quite happy to experiment, because he has no reason to expect a negative reaction. Instead he can develop these behaviours freely. He will try out different ways to establish which behaviour you would like to see, and whether he will get a click or a reward. It is not hard to imagine that cats like that are happy to communicate, perceptive and active. And you are no longer the two-legged tin-opener, but a person to relate to, a friend with whom the cat is able to communicate by using all means available to him. In 2004 some scientists (E. Hiby, E. Rooney, N. and J. Bradshaw) of Bristol University presented a study which investigated the concept of 'positive reinforcement', contrasting it with the concept of punishment in the context of dog training. The results speak for themselves. They clearly demonstrated a positive relationship between obedience and the use of rewards, while the use of punishment was significantly associated with problem behaviour, as for example fear of separation and over-excited behaviour. Human impatience can obviously create its own problems! Dogs and cats are different in many respects, but not in the way they cope with training and upbringing. Positive reinforcement will always be the preferred method for quick and enjoyable learning, and an uninhibited human-animal relationship which is based on mutual trust.

2. Give some thought to each exercise with the clicker before you begin to to work with your cat. Split each action into its separate components, and make a plan for yourself, setting out which part of the action you want to practise and what the result should be. Don't mix the separate criteria! If you want a behaviour to be executed quickly, train for speed, before you practise further criteria. If you have lost your sense of whether you want the cat to lie down for a long or a short period of time, the cat can no longer work out what exactly it is that you want him to do.

3. Keep an open mind and be flexible! Let's assume you are planning to practise lying down with your cat, and instead your cat proffers his paw every time. Just accept the new behaviour that your cat is offering, and schedule the lying down for another day. Please don't be tempted to push the cat down to force him into a lying-down position. If you combine the 'positive reinforcement' (the affirmation from the clicker, upon displaying the desired behaviour) with a 'positive punishment' (by adding an element of force), all you'll get is this: your cat will learn that he isn't free to do what he likes after all, that the click is accompanied by a negative development, and he will no longer dare to experiment and to try things out. All you'll achieve is that, in due course, your cat will probably no longer be willing to cooperate at all any more.

4. If your cat only has eyes for the reward, hide it (the treat, or the toy feather, or whatever) in your closed hand behind your back, or pick it up only once you have made the click. The cat is supposed to concentrate on the action. He'll only get a treat once he's carried out the action. This means: you get nothing for nothing. It's not the treat that influences the action, but the action has an influence on whether or not a reward will follow.

For a difficult exercise, or when dealing with young cats, you can help things along at the beginning by letting a treat roll in the desired direction, thereby making the cat follow it. But please don't get into the habit of luring the cat with a treat. This way, the only progress you make would be imaginary. You'd only be teaching the cat to follow the treat, as opposed to promoting independent trial and error behaviour, and effective work with the clicker. If you work with the clicker in small increments, the amount of dispensed treats can be reduced with time. Luring the cat with a treat simply doesn't work. Luring with a treat is characterised by the fact that the treat is shown before the click. The correct sequence of events, however, is this: first the click – then the reward!

5. As soon as you've reached the stage where the execution of an action is working really well, and you have assigned a name to the whole thing – such as for instance 'Sit!' – please make sure you only say it once. Don't repeat the word two, three or four times. The cat will only learn that you say everything several times over. Ask the cat to sit down. If he doesn't sit down, put the clicker and the reward to one side and just walk away. Your cat is learning according to the 'trial and error' principle. And this way he will remember that he only has one chance per click.

6. Because the cat makes an association between everything that happens simultaneously, it is important to check every now and then which stimuli he has associated with the trained action. Are you sure that it really is the command 'Sit!' that he responds to? Or is it rather a specific movement which you have subconsciously made every time, such as, for example, reaching for the treat? Next time when you ask your cat to sit, try and move as little as possible. Does he understand the word? Or will he not react all of a sudden?

With cats who are deaf, it is important to always make the same distinct movement. This way you avoid misunderstandings and retain the enjoyment of learning, for your cat and for yourself. Also bear in mind that your cat may possibly already have associated the act of sitting down with something else beforehand. If he happens to have shaken his head a couple of times at precisely the moment when you made the click, it is quite possible that the cat is now of the opinion that the exercise requires him to sit down and shake his head two times. Sometimes really grotesque habits can creep in, and at some point you may ask yourself, why on earth is the cat doing this thing? Watch carefully! If everything has gone to plan, you'll get the following result: a term, or rather, a command,

will always trigger the same behaviour in a cat. The cat will display this behaviour without exception upon expressly being given the command (except for the possibility that the cat may sit down without pursuing a treat). The cat only receives a click and a reward if a command has actually been given.

7. You'll remember the first exercise, for which I had suggested, by way of an exception, to click 'into the void'. You should never coax or call your cat towards you with the clicker. If you do that, you will be wasting the clicker as a teaching implement. There will be no conditioning at all, because it is impossible for you to know what exactly you have just affirmed with the click. Let's assume your cat is roaming out of doors, and it is time for him to come home. If you were to stand in front of your front door and beckon the cat to come home by using the clicker, what might actually happen is that the cat is at that precise moment walking away from the house. Or he is drinking ice-cold milk from the fridge which the nice, but misguided, lady next door is always giving him, and which regularly gives him diarrhoea at home – and this is the behaviour that you have just affirmed with a click!

8. Make sure from the start that, in his enthusiasm, the cat doesn't display any rough manners towards you. Don't allow your cat to get carried away, and to bite or whack you when you're giving him his treat. Terminate the training instantly as soon as your cat displays any uncouth behaviour. This kind of behaviour becomes ingrained quicker than you may think, and it is very difficult to get the cat to unlearn such behaviour later on.

'Come home!'

Do you own one of those little vagabonds, who shamelessly and on a regular basis ignore the rules regarding homecoming times? Are you wellknown in your neighbourhood for constantly being on the look-out for your little gypsy? If so, you have two options: either you acquire the nerves of steel that characterise the owner of an outdoor roaming cat, and learn not to get worked up about it, or you try and teach the little tramp to come to you when you call him. As mentioned above, regular feeding times tend to prove very useful for this.

Begin at home in your house by affirming spontaneous behaviour: if you notice that your cat is about to approach you anyway, call his name and click once while the cat is walking towards you. As soon as he has reached you, give him a reward. Take the exercise to the next level by calling the cat – but please, only once! If the cat doesn't put in an appearance, he will miss out on the reward. If he does turn up, you click once while he is approaching you, and give him another treat. At the beginning, don't call the cat when there is little probability of him showing up, for example when he is engaged in deep and peaceful slumber, or watching the birds chattering from behind the window pane. As I have already described, you shape the exercise for a speedy execution. Gradually increase the distance that the cat has to cover in order to reach you, as well as the exposure to external distractions.

Of course the whole thing will work only when you get into the habit of only using the cat's name when you actually want something from him. If your cat hears his name called a hundred times a day, but you have called him to come to you only twice, your cat would indeed have to possess mind-reading powers in order to be able to tell whether his name means that he is being called to come to you, or not. For the purpose of everyday chats, you could always give your little moggy a nickname which would not have the characteristics of a signal.

The handshake and household chores

Learning the handshake provides the foundation for the cat working with his paws. Your little furry household assistant is able to shut drawers, possibly open them too, depending on how they're made, operate easy-to-reach lightswitches, and learn to do many other tasks. All these exercises are designed to combat boredom, and are fun for human and cat alike. Begin by having your cat sit down. Put a treat in your hand and hold it under the cat's nose.

As soon as the cat approaches the treat with his head, you move a small distance away from the cat, and slowly describe a quarter circle around the cat's head. Will he get up in order to follow the treat? Then you ask him once more to assume the 'sit' position and try the same thing again. By following the treat with his head, the cat will end up in a slightly bowed-over sideways position, a movement which takes a little weight off the opposite

*When practising the 'punch', the tumbler
has to be whacked with gusto.*

*Anima is busy practising to operate a light switch
which has been mounted on a piece of cardboard.*

front leg. The slightest reduction of weight on the leg is reason enough for you to make a click. Gradually the cat will come to understand that the click has something to do with taking the weight off one of his front paws, or the lifting of a paw.

Hot-headed go-getters will soon attempt to grasp the hand containing the treat, and dangle after it. This too is an action that warrants a click, because the criterion for the handshake is first of all lifting a front leg off the ground. But make sure right from the start that you only give the click if the claws are retracted! After all, we don't want to train our little moggy to develop into a thug. As always, as soon as the cat has mastered the

exercise, the click is preceded with a command, which could be 'Handshake!' or – if you want to be totally with-it: 'Gimme five!' This way, once the cat has learned to employ his paws following a command, a whole variety of different things can be practised.

You can also find many things which a cat can operate in toyshop departments normally serving toddlers' play and learning needs.

If a cat is learning to operate a lightswitch, you should work with a switch that is lying on the floor at first. You can mount the lightswitch on a cardboard box, lean this construction against a wall, and then gradually hang it higher and higher, until you have reached the height of a real lightswitch. Of

Sometimes patience is needed – and perhaps an intensive talk – in order to persuade the cat to join in.

Moses is having the lever mechanism of the treat dispenser explained to him, with a demonstration.

The first attempt, and it's working quite well already! With the help of shaping, Moses will learn to push down the lever himself and operate the treat dispenser unaided.

course the cat has to be able to reach the lightswitch somehow, by jumping on a chest of drawers or a sofa, for example. You see – a cat can illuminate your life in more than one way!

Playing rough and 'without claws'

Chasing prey is a crucial part of cat's play. This is about practising for the real thing, and all the associated movements will be rehearsed to perfection. It would therefore make sense for the toy to imitate the prey as closely as possible. Prey scurries away, cowers in a corner, waits for an opportunity to escape, hides from the patiently waiting cat. Prey doesn't tend to leisurely saunter around the room, but instead it moves away from the cat with swift, darting movements. In order for your cat to be able to fully enjoy his playtime, this is the way you should act with the cat toy, as well. But please don't torment the cat with the toy. I have never observed a mouse springing an attack on my cat as he was walking across the garden.

Now there are a few feline delinquents who will always go for the human hand, in spite of our attempts to play a proper hunting game with them. Before the next playing session, equip yourself with a clicker. If the little ruffian doesn't accept your offer of a game with a toy dangling from the end of a rod, but is only watching the movements of your hand instead, you just break off the playing session. After a few minutes, you can start a fresh attempt. Is he using his claws against you? If

he is, just break off the playing sessions without a comment. But if he begins to concentrate on the toy offered by you, he will get a click. This is followed by a reward by way of a boisterous playing session.

You can deal with any rough behaviour displayed by your cat towards you in the same fashion. As soon as the claws come out, you terminate any interaction. Affirm every action not involving claws with a click, and in due course, you can add – as before – the command: 'No claws!'.

Cats who make it their hobby to hide behind doors in order to ambush their owner's legs are often under-employed and plain bored. The little leg-biter has realised that after launching such an attack, he will at last get your full attention. Whether this attention consists of you screaming in pain, or scolding, or diverting his attention away from your legs with a toy (thus rewarding the attack, on top of everything else), is of secondary importance. Attention is attention, no matter whether it's negative or positive. Make it a habit to hold daily playing sessions, with the specific aim of keeping your little fighter occupied. How about a game of clicker? Don't leave the cat toys lying around, so they won't lose their attraction. Enrich the cat's environment with tree trunks brought into the house, with cardboard boxes filled with silk paper, an aromatic piece of moss, or an occasional rearranging of the scratching tree. Counteract the boredom and save your cat much frustration and potential problem behaviour.

Developing chains of behaviour

As the name suggests, this involves a whole range of different behaviour. Even small chains of behaviour should be recognised as such. If, for example you call your cat, and he is supposed to come to you, jump on a stool and sit down, then that's a chain of behaviour. The cat is supposed to always react in the same manner. And there are three or four different actions which have to be learned separately: coming to you, jumping up, sitting down, and possibly also waiting.

The chain of behaviour:
Various actions are carried out in a rigid and constant sequence. The affirmation via a click is given only when all the separate actions have been completed. Each individual part of the action triggers the subsequent part of the action and does not require a separate command. Once the first part of the action has been initiated, all the other actions automatically follow. For this reason, when training chains of behaviour you should always begin with the action at the end of the chain, because this is the driving force behind the cat's motivation. Only after the final part has been completed does the cat get his reward.

Take the following example: you want your cat to voluntarily go to the cat basket and lie down inside it, following a specific command. If you divide this into its separate components, you'll get the following individual actions: walking towards the basket, entering it and lying down inside it (as well as, in due course, remaining inside it for a certain amount of time). At first sight, this might appear to be easy, but the tricky part is that the cat actually has to walk away from you – and thus from the reward – in order to

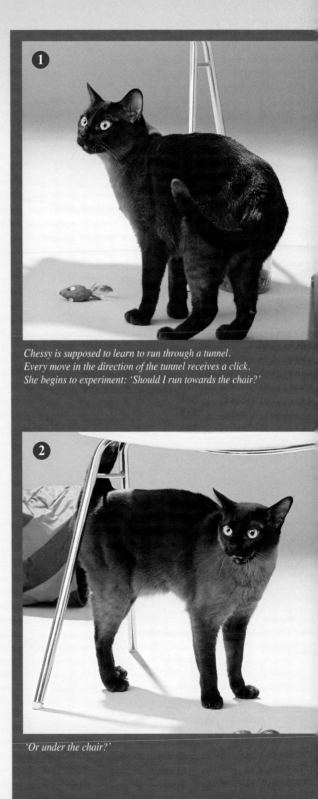

Chessy is supposed to learn to run through a tunnel. Every move in the direction of the tunnel receives a click. She begins to experiment: 'Should I run towards the chair?'

'Or under the chair?'

3

'*Or even on top of the chair?*'

4

Chessy has discovered the tunnel and looks surprised, because she has received a click just for looking at it.

5

Chessy is thinking: 'It's got to have something to do with this thing over there', and receives another click for approaching the tunnel.

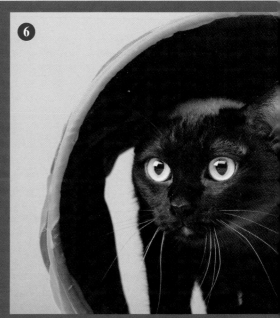

6

Chessy has understood and is now inside the tunnel.

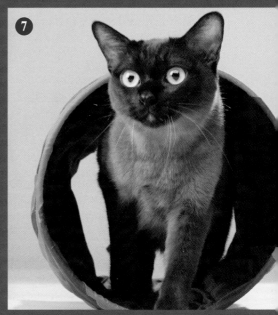

7

Made it! Well done!

get to the basket. You may have guessed how it starts: with the final part of the chain of behaviour, which involves the cat learning to lie down. Where exactly doesn't matter at the beginning. But now the lying down becomes a segment in a chain of behaviour, and he is supposed to learn to lie down inside the basket.

If your cat doesn't normally go into the cat basket voluntarily, something that is frequently the case with animals who associate negative experiences with the basket, such as car rides or visits to the vet, from now on the treats will only be available in and around the hated basket. Leave the transport container some-where in the house in an open and accessible place, so the cat will become used to seeing it there, and understand that he doesn't have to run away from it. If your cat is suspicious even before anything has happened, limit his escape route by closing the doors to other rooms, and busy yourself with doing some-thing else (reading the paper, watching TV, or whatever). At some point the cat will realise that there is something missing in the se-quence of events he had stored in his head. Because if the point of the exercise was a visit to the vet, then you would have tried to grab kitty by now. But that's not what you do. If your cat emerges from his hiding place full of suspicion, please don't talk to him. Wait patiently to see what will happen. Will the cat make a few tentative steps towards the transport basket? Fantastic! Click and reward! In the early stages you can roll the treats on the floor towards the cat.

Give a click for even the tiniest sign of an approach that the cat makes towards the transport basket. Be prepared for your cat to look at you with a baffled expression: 'What on earth was that click for?'. But because he already knows the clicker, he will begin to experiment, because he would like to receive some more clicks and some more rewards too. Does he sit down? Show no reaction. If the cat remains stubbornly sitting down, take a treat and let it roll in the direction of the transport basket. Will the cat get up in order to collect the treat? Good! A click and a reward! You're only giving your cat a little bit of assistance. Now wait and see what the cat will do. Do we have to help him along with a further treat, or will he take another step towards the basket? Click and treat! Does he even nudge the basket with his nose? That's absolutely brilliant! Give the cat a click and a whole little pile of treats, and take the basket away. (It is very important to make the basket disappear at this point. If you leave it there, it is possible that the cat may approach it once more without you noticing, while you are busy doing something else. This would be frus-trating for the cat, because no click would be forthcoming.) After this you should pack it in; you've done enough for the first day.

If you repeat this exercise daily, you will find that within a very brief period of time the cat will be eagerly walking back and forth between you and the basket in order to get his treat. Only proceed to the next stage once this part is working really well. Now it is no longer enough for your cat to walk towards the

This is about entering the transport basket.
First Chessy puts a front paw inside.

The whole cat is inside the transport basket.

Then both front paws!

Turning around inside the basket …

Chessy has three paws in the basket already.

…and finally 'Sit!' Chessy has mastered
the whole chain of behaviour.

transport basket, he will have to touch the basket as well, one way or another, with his nose or with his paw. Increase the amount of tasks involved slowly and gradually, but steadily. During the following days one paw ought to find its way into the transport basket, then both front paws and so forth, until the entire cat is inside the basket. But this piece of the chain of behaviour has to be mastered with confidence, before you add the last part (or actually what was originally the first part). Only then add the already familiar command 'Lie down!' And when the whole sequence of events has been running without any problem several days in a row, you have to give a name to the whole chain of behaviour, such as, for example 'Into the basket!', or 'Get in!'. (This exercise can also be trained with a target stick – we'll come to this later.)

You can practise many other things in the same way as this chain of behaviour, using the cat flap for example, doing 'fetch', or memorising a complicated, but always identical, way home for roaming outdoor cats. Before each session with the clicker, please take time to think about one thing: what exactly do I want to achieve? Are we dealing with a simple action, or does it consist of several smaller actions? If it is a chain of behaviour, which is the final segment, the part I have to start with?

'Fetch!'

Don't worry – I'm not getting things confused here! I really do mean cats, and not dogs!

Some cats fetch objects such as toy mice, small balls, corks or similar items by themselves, but they can also be specifically taught to do so. It is, however, an advanced exercise for human and animal alike. You will shortly see why. And then you will understand why so few dogs are able to 'fetch' properly.

'Fetch' is a chain of behaviour, because it consists of several different actions: picking up an object, holding onto the object, coming towards the owner whilst carrying the object, and finally letting go of the object.

Step 1: As soon as your playful moggy happens to have an object in his mouth, you make a click. (Please don't forcibly stuff an object into the cat's mouth for this purpose!) Once more, I remind you that the click is ending the action! A cat who is already familiar with the clicker will drop the object on the ground in any case, because he is expecting a reward from you after the click. Thus we have the first part of the chain of behaviour, 'Fetch', which will come to represent its conclusion in the end. You don't have to do anything apart from giving your cat a click when he has an object in his mouth. Because the practised clicker cat is inventive, he will try to find out which behaviour has been rewarded with the click. But under no circumstances make the click if the cat is merely looking at the toy mouse, or touching it with his paw. That would take you into the field of targeting, and the cat would be unable to distinguish between the different exercises. Just be prepared at all times, and as soon as you observe that the cat has something in his mouth, give him a click. This will prompt kitty to increasingly carry his favourite toy mouse around with him.

Step 2: Use the shaping technique in order to increase the time for which an object is held in the mouth. The click is just given later, and the time that elapses until the click is made will gradually be increased by tiny increments.

Step 3: Afterwards, with the aid of 'shaping', the cat discovers that it is not enough to have and to hold the object in its mouth, but that he has to walk towards you as well. The easiest way of doing this is by moving further and further away from the cat, as soon as he has picked up the object. You only click once the cat is moving towards you with the object in his mouth. First the distances will have to be relatively small, but you can gradually increase them little by little.

Step 4: The next step to be trained is for the cat to learn to take an object in his mouth. Throw kitty a furry toy mouse. (A cat is interested in everything that moves, which means we are affirming a spontaneous behaviour.) Give a click for following the toy mouse, or even any move towards it.

Step 5: Join the separately trained action segments together. You throw the toy mouse, which the cat will follow and pick up, then he'll move towards you, or rather come to you, in order that he can drop the mouse and receive a reward.

Step 6: Now start to assign a name to the action. If you have no aversion to dog games, how about 'Fetch!'? As always, the command is given before the action is carried out, and before the click.

It is advisable to pick one particular 'fetch' object, and to tidy this away outside practisce time. This is because if the cat carries an object and doesn't get a click, he'll get frustrated. Also the object concerned will not lose its attractiveness as quickly. If a new object is involved, the cat has to learn to fetch this new object from scratch, but because he already knows the procedure, it doesn't take long before he is able to fetch this and other things as well. The super-professionals among clicker cats can finally also learn what the individual objects are called, and they will be able to fetch the 'mouse', the (catnip) bag, and many other specific objects.

Developing sequences of behaviour

When practising sequences of behaviour, we are actually dealing with a chain of behaviour as well, the difference being that there isn't a rigid order in which the actions have to be carried out. You tell or show the cat which bit of the action he should do next. You will need to employ this method, for example, when you install an obstacle course for your cat to negotiate. You can have the cat walk across high boards, through tunnels (folded open paper bags will do), or a seesaw, around obstacles in his path, jump on a stool, etc. Each obstacle is practised individually. It doesn't matter where you begin, because at every obstacle you have to tell the cat what he is supposed to do. You give each obstacle

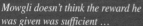

Mowgli doesn't think the reward he was given was sufficient ...

... and is serving himself.

hold the target again in the same place. Make sure that at the beginning, the distance between the cat and the target stick is really small. Always hold the target stick sideways to the cat, never with the tip pointing straight towards the cat, because one small surprise move, and the cat may be injured. Approach with the target stick from the left, as well as from the right side, so the cat will get used to both situations. If the cat ignores the target stick, move it around a little in order to attract the cat's attention to the stick. If the cat is very cautious and doesn't dare to touch the target stick, at the beginning you can give a click as soon as the cat takes a look at the stick. But with every new attempt, always give the cat a fresh opportunity to touch the target stick with his nose. Very important: briefly take the target stick away after each click, before presenting it once more. Increase the level of difficulty. After a few exercises the cat is supposed to not just touch the

The target stick is showing Moses what the next exercise is called: 'jump on the chair'.

Moses knows that his task has not been completed, because the target hasn't disappeared yet.

target stick anywhere, but only on the tip of the stick. So you only give a click if the tip of the target stick has actually been touched. Once this works without any problems, it's time for the next criterion, which is: the cat is supposed to stay with his nose touching the stick for a prolonged period of time. As described with regard to 'shaping', you only

affirm the longest nose-to-target-stick-tip touching moments, and increase their duration gradually. Don't forget: the click ends the exercise and allows the cat to remove his nose from the target stick. You can also add a command to this exercise ('Touch nose!', or 'Touch!', for example). This part of the target training is a very good

First he's got to pretend to be a dangerous panther …

… and after the target stick has indicated to him 'jump off the chair', it disappears, and Moses receives a click and a reward.

exercise especially for cats who tend to find it hard to control their temper at times, because this way they learn to concentrate and keep in control of themselves.

Once you have achieved this, you can begin to slightly move the target stick away from the cat, so he is forced to follow the target stick in order for his nose to stay in contact with the tip. Increase the distance over which your cat is supposed to follow the target stick. This is when a telescopic target stick comes in handy, because you can walk upright as the cat is following it.

Now you can think about what you want to do next. Do you want your cat to climb up a ladder, crawl under an obstacle or through a tunnel, or walk across a wooden board? Take yourself and your cat to the obstacle which you have constructed earlier, give the command 'Nose!' or 'Touch!' – or whatever name you want to give this exercise – and present the target stick. Guide the cat through or across the obstacle, and gradually increase the level of difficulty. The aim is to be able to produce a click at precisely the moment when the cat has overcome the obstacle. These kinds of achievements are best rewarded with a jackpot.

After a few repetitions the cat knows what he has to do, and you can give a name to the completed chain of actions (i.e. touching the target stick with the nose, staying in touch with the target stick, following the target stick and walking across the wooden board at the same time – altogether four different components!). Finally you could perhaps add the command 'Sit!', which kitty can already do to perfection by now (which would make 'sit' the first, or rather the last, part of the chain of behaviour!). Click and reward!

If you set up several obstacles which have to be negotiated one by one, each of them has to be trained separately. Every obstacle involves a chain of behaviour. If you want to alter, change and vary the sequence in which the obstacles are to be overcome every time, the cat needs a separate command in order to tell him what has to be done next, which makes this a sequence of behaviour.

Of course, up to now this has just been pure sporting fun, but one day, upon finding your moggy whining his heart out atop a tree or on the neighbour's balcony (who has possibly gone away on a long holiday) because he is too scared to come down again, then you'll be more than happy that your cat has been trained to follow a target stick, and walk down a ladder or a wooden board which is leaning against a wall, or to climb nonchalantly into the proferred cat basket. The target stick to the rescue!

Going for walks together

You can also use the target stick in order to practise going for walks together – with or without a harness. First you give a click for the cat tolerating the harness as described above, and then for accepting a leash to be attached to it, which means a reduced radius of movement for the cat. You must remain calm and patient while doing this, because this is a completely new feeling for the cat, and he has to get used to the fact that he can't just run away. You can help the cat by distracting him and by starting to use the target stick. Instead of panicking and throwing himself against the leash, the cat can concentrate on following the target stick and learning that things aren't as bad as they might seem. Gradually you proceed to greater challenges: the distance that has to be covered, and the external factors distracting the cat. At the beginning, you click every time the cat walks with you nicely. With the click the target stick disappears, and he'll get a reward. As soon as the cat pulls against the leash, starts to buck, or wanders off in any direction willy-nilly, you just stop walking. The goal you aim for is that the click will only be given at the end of your joint excursion, once you have arrived back home.

Problems with fear

Some cats suffer from anxieties bordering on panic – of strangers, slippery floors, or even of large shopping bags, and I mean it when I say: these animals really do suffer! Their fears are usually the result of a lack of socialisation, genetic predisposition, or bad experiences. Even if we ourselves are able to live with the fact that the cat disappears like greased lightning as soon as a stranger walks through the front door, the cat is actually suffering real stress! Please be aware of this possibility, giving some thought to whether it might be worth the effort to try and help your little darling. You have a tool which you can work with. Now all you need is a little time, and a little more patience. I'm not able to describe every possible situation in detail within the confines of this book, therefore I'll use the frequently occurring fear of visitors as an example. It doesn't matter what other fears and anxieties a cat suffers from, the characteristic behaviour is always the same.

A vital part of the desensitisation (dealing with the fear) is to know what a frightened cat looks like! This is because you have to affirm the correct behaviour, which in this case is not being scared. If you click at the wrong moment, you may actually affirm the fearful reaction, and reinforce it! This can be pure palpable fear, which is hard to miss, because the cat's eyes are wide open with panic, and he will back away, or try and hide. It might also be a considerably less dramatic defensive posture. Defence is the opposite of attack. Here, however, you also have to err on the side of caution. If the cat's escape route is blocked, and he is cornered, he may have no other option than to fight his way out, and the body signals may quite easily tilt in the direction of an attack. Fear and aggression – these two terms are inseparably linked together, because one can trigger the other, and the borders are fluid.

Let's assume that the cat is displaying clear signs of fear, and you have identified these correctly. He will try to escape, back away, push himself into a corner, he will make himself small, pinning his ears backwards to either side of his head, so they almost disappear. He crouches down in order to protect the sensitive parts of his body, such as the neck and tummy region. He may also spit and hiss, his fur standing on end with tension.

Begin the training with the target stick as described above, and have your cat touch the tip of the target stick for a prolonged period of time. This should be done in circumstances free from stress and distraction. Just be very clear about one thing: it doesn't matter which type of fear you are trying to alleviate, you give a click for the touching, and staying in touch with the target stick. This is an important marker for you, otherwise you may run the risk of awarding the click for reacting in a fearful manner. As soon as you have decided that you want to use the target stick to overcome your cat's fear, you should also train other things at the same time, which have nothing to do with stress, and which you do just for the fun of it. Your cat should not end up associating the clicker training exclusively with fear!

Fear of strangers

As soon as kitty has mastered the target practice, has achieved a few successes and has had a few positive experiences with the clicker, ask a neighbour or a friend over for a cup of tea or coffee, in order to provide assistance. Shut the doors to the bedroom, or all those rooms which the cat would definitely use to hide in, but leave enough rooms accessible to him to give him the opportunity to keep the safe distance he desires. (For instance, close the bedrooms, but leave the kitchen and living room open.) Let's assume your visitor is sitting in the living room and the cat has fled into the kitchen. Give him a little time in order to calm himself. Of course it is conducive to the success of the exercise – depending on how scared your little darling is – if the visitor remains quiet, just sits there, and doesn't look at the cat. If your cat doesn't manage to concentrate on the target stick the first time round, don't worry. He will have learnt

something, namely: 'There is a stranger sitting over there, I'm relatively close to her, but nothing bad is happening to me.' The next time, or maybe the time after, things are likely to improve. You already know by now how quickly your cat is able to learn. On no account pay any attention to any signs of fear displayed by your moggy! (Don't comfort, don't touch, don't stare at him! But don't make a click either!)

Let's assume that by now your cat will have relaxed enough to be prepared to go into the kitchen with you (possibly still out of the stranger's sight), to do the targeting procedure and to accept treats. Then you shorten the telescopic target stick, and start using it close to the cat. You gradually lengthen the target stick again and use it to point in the direction of the stranger. The criteria that the cat has to fulfil are: to touch the target stick with his nose and to stay like that until you have made the click. Then follow this by the reward, and don't forget to remove the target stick again after the click. Don't ever give a click to your cat for casting an anxious look towards the visitor. Never give a click if your cat flinches nervously either. Only touching the target stick with his nose warrants a click!

As the training is getting more advanced, the distance between you and the tip of the target stick is getting greater, and this way you slowly work your way out of the kitchen into the sitting room. Don't lose your patience, and gradually advance your training in small steps, ending each exercise with a success for the cat and a jackpot. Make sure that the cat can withdraw (open a bedroom door) when the visitor gets up to leave. The presence of a stranger is enough for your little kitty to deal with. It would be premature to confront him with a stranger who's moving about as well!

It is very useful to invite various helpers into the house, men and women. This is because the cat isn't just supposed to get used to one human being, but also to the fact that visitors are a mundane occurrence; they stay, and they leave again afterwards.

Once you have reached the sitting room with your ongoing target stick training, and you and kitty are about two metres away from your visitor, it's time for the visitor to take over the target stick, while the cat is working with it. As ever, the cat must not be stared at, but the visitor can now begin to briefly glance at the cat, and to squint emphatically (meaning: 'My intentions towards you are friendly') and then look away again. Now the target stick is gradually shortened again, until the cat is in close proximity to the visitor. After getting this far, the biggest mistake anyone could make now would be for the stranger to bow down to the cat in order to stroke him. Any further rapprochement has to be initiated by the cat. He may sniff the visitor's trouser leg (click!) or look at the visitor from a short distance without any signs of fear or anxiety (click!) – the visitor remains absolutely passive. By doing so, in a manner of speaking, the visitor herself becomes the target stick! The cat is allowed to retreat at any time, before the visitor gets up to leave.

As the training progresses the visitor can be given the task of presenting the cat with his jackpot, i.e. (gently!) throwing the furry toy mouse or putting the food bowl in front of the cat. If your cat's primary reinforcer is cuddling, the visitor can begin to passively let her hand dangle downwards. If the cat brushes against it or even rubs himself against it, the visitor may venture to tentatively touch the cat for the first time. They should do this with the back of their hand (this signals: 'Don't worry, I'm not going to try and grab you').

It is not necessary to practise this every day; you will make the best progress, however, by holding small, brief practice sessions several times a day. Anything your cat has learned in this manner will never be lost again. It is important that the cat has no negative experiences during this desensitisation training, such as a visitor who is not involved with the training, storming into the flat. You'll just have intercept unexpected guests at the front door. Maybe you'll be able rope them into assisting you?

It is possible the cat will show renewed fear after the training has been interrupted for several days. But each time the cat will overcome his fear a little more rapidly. Now you'll probably think: 'Good heavens! This is going to take for ever!'. But please don't forget: each practice sequence takes only two to five minutes. That's all! With every success your cat will open up a little more and feel more secure. And if you look at it this way: even if this takes you a few weeks – that's nothing compared to the whole of a cat's lifetime!

Fear of objects

You deal with your cat's fear of objects in much the same way as with unfamiliar human beings. The advantage is that that you can use objects whenever and however it's convenient to you, and they don't usually move either. You help the cat approach the object of fear by making him concentrate on the target stick, and you affirm any contact the cat may engage in with the object of his fear, even if that contact consists only of a hesitant dab of a paw, or even a tentative sniff. To give you a rough generalisation (I'm running the risk that some researchers into feline behaviour may scream in protest at this point, but I just want to give you a hint): only give a click when the the ears are pointing forwards with their open side, meaning that the basic mood is 'neutral'.

Make sure you regularly use different variations of the exercise! The visitor should not always sit in the same spot. Don't always use the same starting point for the exercise! The colour of the plastic bag much feared by your cat should vary, sometimes it should be lying flat on the ground, sometimes more or less full, perhaps it might be suspended from a door handle on occasion, or be placed on a chair. Remember to tidy the 'object of fear' away as soon as the exercise has finished.

Fear of being touched

Perhaps you have taken pity on a poor little moggy from a cat home, but aren't able to touch him yet, after having a got him home safely. The procedure is in principle the same as before, except that to begin with, you use the telescopic target stick extended to its full length, and you roll the treats gently towards the cat (please, no bombardment!), then get him to move closer to you by steadily retracting the target stick. In this case the same rules apply as described above in regard to visitors: don't look or stare at the cat, let your gaze travel around the room in a laid-back manner, squint at him, and only touch the cat if he himself is ready to engage in physical contact with you.

When doing desensitisation work with the clicker, it is crucial to continually give rewards, every click has to be followed by a reward. Every fear-free reaction from the cat has to be affirmed. This could involve touching the target stick (instead of running away, the cat takes advantage of the alternative behaviour offered by the target stick), or the slightest approach towards the object of fear (the cat is learning to overcome his fear).

Cancelling

Cancelling an unwanted behaviour is accomplished by making an existing association disappear gradually, until it has been completely eliminated. We'll stay with the subject of fear of strangers: in this case, for example, the cat has learnt that visitors are a bad thing. Perhaps the reason is that the cat once was chased by boisterous children, or maybe he simply has never learnt to deal with human strangers, or somebody has once inadvertently hurt him, or held him against his will. He will have reacted to this behaviour by withdrawing. It is possible that on top of this, his fear has been affirmed by being coerced into tolerating the touch of strangers, or by being comforted for his fear. The longer this state of affairs has gone on, the longer it will take to achieve cancellation.

Photos 1–6: Getting familiar with a new family member from a different species:

Mowgli is supposed to be taken to meet the dog Monello. For the safety of both parties, he is kept inside a cage to begin with. Step by step, the dog and the cat are made to approach each other with the help of the target stick.

Monello touches the target stick. The distance to the cage is still quite considerable.

Now it's Mowgli's turn.

Gradually the distance between the two is being reduced and the dog is displaying various different body postures, giving the cat an opportunity to get to know the way he moves.

While the cage door is being opened for the cat, the dog is secured on a leash and kept busy with the target stick and clicker.

There must not be any mishaps during this first encounter! When Mowgli fixates the dog in a rather forward manner, the eye contact is briefly interrupted and the cat is distracted.

If this association 'visitor = flight' is worked on by using desensitisation training, it will gradually lessen and weaken, until it has been extinguished. Figuratively speaking, the key (visitor) doesn't fit the lock (flight) any more, and this leads to the cat changing his behaviour. Extinction has nothing to do with forgetting! The previous pairing is replaced by another, preferably positive, association (every time visitors come into the house, something nice happens: treat and

clicker training). This can be achieved reliably and in the shortest possible time by continually affirming every neutral, fear-free stance displayed by the cat.

But be prepared for one thing: before the extinction takes place, the previous behaviour, the fear, will stage a final appearance, and with reinforcements. This is a perfectly normal process! During this time, which will only last a few days, the cat should be allowed to do exercises with a guaranteed

Success! A jackpot for both!

success rate. Some cats get very annoyed and impatient during this period, because they feel the treats they receive are no adequate reward for their performance. Finish the exercise with a particularly fine jackpot, because we can only have a very small inkling of the huge leap of faith this brave little cat's heart is having to perform before our very eyes. Once the extinction has been completed you will be astonished by the progress that your moggy will be making from this point onwards!

Moving away from the reward, in order to receive a reward

Do you have the impression that your cat has only got his beady little eyes on the reward? Is sweet little Tigger too overly keen, and literally performing somersaults when he hears the clicker? Or does Tiddles get all out of control, becoming overexcited? Then I know just the right kind of exercise to calm things down again!

Having to move away from the reward in order to get a reward, here it even involves a chain of behaviour. Mowgli has to walk towards a cone …

… touch it …

... and return ...

... in order to get his reward at the end.

Show your cat, as described above, that he can touch the tip of the target stick (or stick-like implement) with his nose in order to receive a click. But instead of asking your little rascal to stay attached to the target stick with his nose, have him commute between the stick and the treat, back and forth. Take the target stick and the clicker in one hand and the reward (if necessary, hidden behind your back) in the other. Gradually increase the distance between the target stick and the proffered treat! Once you are at your maximum arm's reach, you can then put the stick in a vase or a glass, in order to be able to move still further away from it.

The aim is for kitty to walk up to the target stick and to touch it with his nose. This is the moment you make a click. The cat will rush towards you in order to receive his justly deserved reward. Don't underestimate the difficulty of this training! After all, the cat has to move away from you and the reward, in order to get the reward. But be prepared; within a very short space of time your little moggy will be darting back and forth between the two.

Aggressive behaviour towards humans, dogs and other cats

In order to 'un-train' aggression – similar to the fear training – there is one crucial pre-requisite. You have to be able to recognise the point at which your cat is displaying aggression, so that you'll never inadvertently affirm aggressive behaviour with a click. How successful you'll eventually be depends to a large degree on how carefully you observe your cat's body language! Just because a cat hisses doesn't necessarily mean that he is close to mounting an attack. A cat who really is bent on pure aggression displays offensive behaviour which is threatening an attack. He will make himself appear large by making the fur on his body and on the root of the tail stand on end, with the tail itself pointing downwards in a hook-like shape. He will display his threatening broad side, fixing his gaze on the opponent. The whiskers are fanned out pointing forward. This posture is announcing a bite, i.e. a real physical attack. The ears are turned round so their back sides are pointing forward. A tiger has a white spot on the back of each ear. Genuine African wild cats have an orange spot in the same place. This marking on the fur bears the characteristics of a signal, and unambiguously conveys that this cat means business. Make a mental note of this image.

By contrast, the basic recipe for your clicker training couldn't be simpler: any aggression will be ignored, leading to the termination of all play or training activities, and every desired behaviour – i.e. peaceful, neutral – will be affirmed with the clicker, and thereby reinforced.

Just as with the overcoming of fear and anxiety, here too, it is important that the behaviour that is to be learned, i.e. being peaceful, is generalised. This means the cat isn't just supposed to behave in a peaceful manner towards the other cat (or the new dog) in the kitchen, but in general and everywhere. Consequently, in order to consolidate it, every anti-aggression exercise has to be repeated in different places and under many different circumstances.

Incompatible behaviour means that you train the cat to adopt a particular behaviour in certain situations which is not compatible with the unwanted behaviour. This new behaviour will make it impossible for the the cat to retain his old behaviours.

Because the new behaviour is rewarded, it will be displayed more frequently by the cat. The old behaviour leads to being ignored, and will gradually disappear. Training incompatible behaviour is a genuine alternative to conventional punishment.

Let us suppose you want to integrate a new pet into the family, and your cat's reactions range from curt and unfriendly to really hostile. Proceed in a similar manner as you did with the problem of fear and anxiety. Offer an incompatible behaviour to your cat, and reward any interaction which is free from aggression.

You assign a task to the cat, for example with the aid of training with the target stick. Again, as a prerequisite for this the cat has to already have experienced clicker training in a positive sense. If he only ever experiences it in connection with problem situations, it will soon assume a notion of being rather tiresome. If the cat gets to know the clicker in a positive context, he is completely and utterly unable to engage with the target and be aggressive at the same time (incompatible behaviour). In addition, affirm any behaviour, except behaviour involving aggression (counter-conditioning): every time this strange cat or dog appears, something positive happens).

For safety purposes, separate two adjoining rooms with a balcony net or a cat net. One room contains the 'new kid on the block' (the dog or the other cat), the other your established cat. Begin the target training by putting the greatest possible distance between the two. The cat gets a click for every touch of the target stick, but also for any neutral body posture! Carry out short practice sequences several times a day. Conclude each exercise with a success. Endeavour to steadily approach the separation, i.e. the net, in small

Photos 1–13: Meeting between two cats who have never met each other before.

Again the 'rapprochement' is achieved via target training. The same procedure is recommended for cats who have fallen out with each other, and who you want to reunite.

Mowgli is waiting for his first 'rendezvous' inside the half-covered cage.

At first sight Anima seems quite taken.

Shake hands!

Anima doesn't like the targeting too much and prefers to lift her paw …

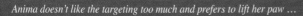

…in order to get a treat. No matter! Every desired behaviour is rewarded, in this case peacefulness.

Mowgli dares to try and fish for a treat which Anima has dropped by mistake.

... and is promptly reprimanded, which leaves him a bit shaken.

It looks as if Anima is trying to help to unlock the cage.

As Mowgli comes out of the cage Anima is still a little tense at being faced with so much self-confidence.

'Bah! You won't impress me by pulling such dare-devil stunts!'

Anima goes into a defensive posture.

But Mowgli doesn't give up and tries his utmost to storm Anima's defences with his youthful impudence.

Communal eating creates a bond, interrupting overly intensive eye contact, and rewarding peaceful behaviour.

steps. As soon as the cat begins to stare at and fixate the 'newbie', you break off the exercise and close the door to the room. Try the same thing again a few hours later. It won't do any harm to proceed in the same way with the other animal too, provided he doesn't feel intimidated.

Outside the clicker practice the door remains closed, but you can change the rooms and their inmates around, so each of them gets the opportunity to familiarise himself with the scent of the other animal.

After you have gradually moved closer to the net, and have managed to keep both animals calm and engrossed in the target training, you should keep things at this level for at least a week. Only then it is time to remove the net. Keep the clicker training going afterwards as well. If you are engaged in clicker training with your old cat, and the newbie joins you, keep going as if nothing had happened, but give the new cat (or dog) a treat after each click as well.

Perhaps doing the familiarisation in this manner will take a little longer. But you'll achieve a real friendship, and not just a mutual toleration. It's definitely worth your while!

Scratching the furniture

Besides the problems with fear and aggression, the one thing that bothers us most of all is cats sharpening their claws in places that aren't meant to be used for this purpose. Cats are not just scratching in order to shed their old claw husks, their main interest is to mark their territory with their own scent. This is the reason why you can observe a contagious effect when there are several cats. As soon as one cat begins to sharpen his claws, another one will quickly join in, and a virtual scratching competition ensues. This is all well and fine, but please not on the new leather sofa! Unfortunately cats have no concept of material values. And if we come skidding around the corner, waving a water squirter, or whatever comes to hand for the protection of our property, this will only make the cat scratch in secret. So what is one to do?

First of all we have to offer the cat an attractive and adequate substitute. The cat should have sufficient opportunities for scratching. Scratching posts or trees that are covered with sisal are more popular than those covered with carpet. On one hand the material has to be soft enough for the cat to be able to dig his claws into the material, but on the other hand, hard enough to offer a feeling of resistance. Vertical scratching implements are usually preferable to horizontal ones. Unfortunately many scratching posts are put in locations which the cat doesn't find very attractive. A scratching post should be placed next to a window, with further scratching implements near the favourite sleeping places. If, in spite of all these improvements, a particular spot in the home remains a preferred scratching place, you can cover it temporarily with plastic sheeting and offer the cat a suitable scratching opportunity next to it. For really obsessive scratching fiends, you can stick double-sided sticky tape all over the plastic sheeting as well (a very unpleasant sensation when the fine hairs between the pads get stuck to it!). Conversely, when the little devil uses the scratching implement provided, he will get a click! This way you are affirming and reinforcing positive be-haviour.

Please remember: scratching the furniture can also assume the characteristics of an attention-grabbing exercise. Once the little kitty has learnt that he'll only get your attention by pulling such stunts, this sort of behaviour
produces a rewarding effect in two respects. You are paying attention to the cat (even if it is the negative kind), and at the same time he is marking his territory. Once more, playing and clicker exercises offer an alternative by keeping the cat occupied with other things.

Special questions

Clicker training involving several cats

You can use a clicker even when there are several cats living in the same household. The conditioning and the learning of new behaviour should be done individually, however, so that you can be sure that each cat has understood what's expected of him, and is able to put it into practice. While you're working with one animal, the others should be shut away.

After this you have several alternatives. Either you train with each cat whatever he does best, or whatever he spontaneously displays most often. This way the little live wire of a tom-cat, who is such a skilled climber, can learn, for example, how to run across planks or boards, climb up or down a ladder, or do a high-speed slalom. And with the laid-back little moggy with the temperament of a teddy-bear, you can practise things requiring skill, calm and stamina. For example operating a light-switch, or fishing treats out of a detergent ball, and many more things.

You can do the same exercises with two cats. If another cat joins you while you're busy doing some clicker training with one cat, you'll only give a click to the cat who you're actually working with at the time, but both get a treat for displaying the correct behaviour.

Or you can use different clickers, two- or three-tone clickers, and in due course different words to go with each clicker tone. If you are doing this, it is important, of course, for each cat to know his own specific clicker tone very well, and in addition for you to remember precisely which clicker tone (or which word) you have assigned to which cat respectively.

Because the individual practice sequences shouldn't be overly long anyway, you can teach your cats that whoever is not actively working with you has to lie down and wait. Then after a few minutes it's the other cat's turn.

course you will only have to use the clicker when you want to teach your cat a new behaviour. You can begin to replace the click with a word for exercises that the cat is already very familiar with. Be careful not to use a word which is commonly used in everyday conversation, in order to preserve its function as a signal. The signal can also be a tongue click, or a word or sound such as, for example: 'click', 'si', 'whoops', and many more. Just like a click, the word has to be short, succinct and unambiguous. You have to say your click word within half a second before each click at the most. This sounds familiar, doesn't it? Exactly, we're about to classically condition a word to replace the clicker sound. The procedure is as follows:

➤ Command 'Sit!' > action > click word
> click > reward

Remember that the word has exactly the same function as the click. It concludes the action. Don't use praise words for this purpose. Praise is a primary reinforcer and should only be used following the click – or straight after the click word.

Clicker training without a clicker

Maybe you have been enthusiastic about working with a clicker up to this point – at least I should hope so! But by now you may be wondering whether you will have to carry a clicker on your person for the rest of your life. No, you don't have to do that! In due

Problems with the litter tray

The perennial number one at the top of the chart in the field of behavioural therapies is, and always will be, problems regarding the use of the litter tray. A distinction has to be made between cats who have a problem with toilet training, and those who urine-mark. This usually affects owners of pure indoor cats; but because not everybody has this problem, it cannot be said to be caused principally by the lack of an outdoor roaming opportunity. A majority of the cases are due to a health issue, such as a undiagnosed latent bladder infection. Fellow cats who are not tolerated also often act as a trigger for such problems, but it can also be boredom or attention-grabbing behaviour. This subject is so multi-layered that I could fill an entire book with it, but in order to stay on the subject of clicker training, I'll just give you a brief summary. If there haven't been any obvious changes in the household, if the cat litter brand has not been changed recently, if there are litter trays provided in sufficient numbers (two for the first cat and one further tray for each additional cat), if the cat is being kept sufficiently occupied, played with, and not bored, if the trays are in the correct locations (please don't put them next to the food bowl or next to the favourite sleeping place!), you should take the cat to the vet straight away. I'd recommend the involvement of an expert in the field of animal psychology or behavioural therapy, in order to investigate the root causes, only when any health problems have positively been excluded.

In my opinion, clicker training unfortunately offers no suitable treatment option for this particular problem area. Theoretically you would have to give a click to your cat as soon as he is about to set foot in the litter tray, or is about to use it. But because the click is supposed to end the behaviour, this would cause the cat to hold in his business and leave the tray in order to collect the reward. Cats who use the tray as well as other, undesired places, can be affirmed with the clicker immediately at the point when they are actually using the toilet. If we assume that the cat does his business elsewhere as a 'cry for help' (he may be unwell) or in order to get attention (he may be unhappy, something's amiss), this behaviour will inevitably be reinforced much more, because we effectively give the cat our attention – even if it's just by cleaning up the soiled area.

This should not be confused with terms such as 'pure spite' or 'protest'! If a cat forgets his toilet training, there is always a reason, and you should always try to investigate what's at the bottom of it, instead of just carrying out punitive measures.

To keep it short – in order to repair problems involving the litter tray, the causal factors have to be modified. Unfortunately a clicker will hardly be sufficient here. I dare say, however (admittedly without being able to cite any scientific statistics!) that clicker-trained cats experience far fewer problems of this kind. Unfortunately as yet in Europe there aren't that many cats who undergo clicker training, which means that we don't have the empirical evidence to confirm this.

But you never know! Maybe this book has made a contribution towards turning you into a confirmed clicker fan? Then we shall soon know more about the balanced, fulfilled life of clicker cats! I hope you and your little moggy are going to have a lot of fun together!